HE SAID - I AM
... AND HE IS

HE SAID - I AM
... AND HE IS

Glenn C. Carlson

Copyright © 2020 by Glenn C. Carlson.

Library of Congress Control Number:		2020910735
ISBN:	Hardcover	978-1-9845-8336-9
	Softcover	978-1-9845-8335-2
	eBook	978-1-9845-8334-5

All rights reserved. No part of this book may be reproduced or transmitted in any form or by any means, electronic or mechanical, including photocopying, recording, or by any information storage and retrieval system, without permission in writing from the copyright owner.

The views expressed in this work are solely those of the author and do not necessarily reflect the views of the publisher, and the publisher hereby disclaims any responsibility for them.

Scripture quotations marked NRSV are taken from the New Revised Standard Version of the Bible, Copyright © 1989, by the Division of Christian Education of the National Council of the Churches of Christ in the United States of America. Used by permission. All rights reserved. Website

Any people depicted in stock imagery provided by Getty Images are models, and such images are being used for illustrative purposes only.
Certain stock imagery © Getty Images.

Print information available on the last page.

Rev. date: 06/09/2020

To order additional copies of this book, contact:
Xlibris
1-888-795-4274
www.Xlibris.com
Orders@Xlibris.com
812516

CONTENTS

Jesus: Different? 1

"I Am the Bread of Life" 5

"I Am the Light of the World" 11

"I Am the Gate for the Sheep" 15

"I Am the Good Shepherd" 21

"I Am the True Vine" 27

"I Am the Resurrection and the Life" 33

"I Am the Way, amd the Truth, and the Life" 39

The End? Just the Beginning...45

Addendum 47

Index...49

The Gospel according to John, the Fourth Gospel, could be called a sermon. The unknown author (preacher), sometimes too hastily referred to as the Apostle John, was preaching to Christians around 90–110 CE. This is about seventy to eighty years after Jesus and about thirty to forty years after Mark, Luke, and Matthew (their exact dates are not known). John never directly mentions these Synoptic Gospels with whom it has only about 10 percent similarity.

To make the Fourth Gospel's origin even more complex, we're told that the author is probably only the editor. The author says the real writer is a disciple of Jesus (John 21:24). And then to add to the mystery, we're told that this disciple was "the disciple whom Jesus loved" (John 21:20). Since Jesus loved all of his disciples, the mystery deepens.

The capstone of this enigma is this: the Beloved Disciple only appears during Jesus's last week. He never appears elsewhere in Jesus's life and ministry.

1. He is with the Apostles on the last Thursday night, sitting next to Jesus (John 13:23).
2. He is at the Crucifixion and is asked by Jesus to care for his mother (John 19:26).
3. He goes to the empty tomb with Mary Magdalene and Peter (John 20:2–8).
4. He is with six other disciples fishing at Lake Tiberius and is the first to see Jesus onshore (John 21:7).

5. He also may have been the "other disciple" who was with Peter the Thursday night Jesus was arrested (John 18:15–16).

F. V. Filson in *The Interpreter's Dictionary of the Bible* says, "A final decision [about the Beloved Disciple's identity] is hardly possible."

In addition to the Beloved Disciple, we need to pay attention to the preacher's congregation, the readers. They were Jews who were being kicked out of their synagogues because they had become Christians. They were also Gentiles and Samaritans who had become Christians and didn't always get along with their Jewish Christian neighbors. The preacher and his multifaceted congregation lived in a very hostile environment. The Roman government was in absolute control of Israel. Christians were being crucified and burned on crosses. Rome said that there was only one supreme authority and that was Caesar, not Jesus. The writer of Revelation was exiled to an island for proclaiming otherwise c. AD 95–100.

Being a preacher/pastor in such a belligerent setting would have been very difficult as well as dangerous. He needed to demonstrate to this admixture of Christians that what he said was true. The writer-preacher of the Fourth Gospel knew that he had to speak words that described and explained events that had been witnessed and that were substantiated by God. He was well aware that after the Resurrection, Jesus said that he would be present and testify to the contemporary world in the person of the Holy Spirit. "I have said these things to you while I am still with you. But the Advocate ["helper"], the Holy Spirit, whom the Father will send in my name, will teach you everything, and remind you of all that I have said to you" (John 14:25–26).

In his final appearance, Jesus tells his disciples that he will continue to be with them in the person of the Holy Spirit as they carry on his ministry.

> "As the Father has sent me, so I send you."
> When he had said this, he breathed on them and said to them, "Receive the Holy Spirit. If you forgive the sins of any, they are forgiven them . . ." (John 20:21–23)

The final chapter presents a remarkable possibility. "This is the [Beloved] disciple who is testifying to these things and has written them, and we know that his testimony is true" (John 21:24). *Is it possible that the Beloved Disciple who only appears in this Gospel in the last week of Jesus's life on earth (John 13–21) is the Holy Spirit personified, witnessing to the truth of these events?* It may be that the preacher/author of this Gospel was introducing a nonhistorical personage who never appears in the Synoptic Gospels. He wanted to explain that the Holy Spirit of the risen Christ, appearing as a disciple, was testifying to the reality and truth of everything written/preached in the Fourth Gospel. Jesus would appear not to deny such a possibility when Peter asks concerning the Beloved Disciple, "Lord, what about him?" Jesus replies, "If it is my will that he remain until I come, what is that to you? Follow me!" (John 21:21–22). If such an audacious possibility is true, then this writer/preacher was delivering the Gospel to his congregation in a more courageous, dramatic way than most preachers would dare.

Jesus: Different?

In the Fourth Gospel, we see Jesus presented in a different way than he is in the Synoptic Gospels (Matthew, Mark, and Luke). "What is most characteristic of the Gospel of John is lacking in the Synoptic Gospels, and what is most typical of the Synoptic Gospels cannot be found in John" (*Introducing the New Testament*, Achtemeier, Green, Thompson, p.199). In John, Jesus speaks and acts in a more spiritual, heavenly way than he does in the other Gospels. From the very beginning he is the Word of God, the Son of God who reveals the one true God (John 1:14–18).

In Matthew 20:22, when a mother asks for her two sons to have a special place in the kingdom, Jesus replies, "You don't know what you're asking. Are you able to drink the cup that I'm about to drink?" But in John 18:11, Jesus says, "Am I not to drink the cup that the Father has given me?"

In Mark 6:3, the people say, "Is this not this the carpenter . . . ?" In John 7:28, Jesus says, "I have not come on my own. But the one who sent me is true, and you do not know him."

In John 6:25–59, we find Jesus speaking on a high, heavenly level while the people try to translate his words into plain, understandable conversation. Jesus says, "Do not work for the food that perishes, but for the food that endures for eternal life" (John 6:27). The people, thinking of physical food, ask what they have to do to get it. Jesus maintains his elevated speech, but this time in the third person, "This is the work of God, that you believe in him whom he has sent" (John 6:29).

In this paraphrased dialogue of John 6:25–34, we hear the humanness of the people vis-à-vis the divine humanness of Jesus.

People: We'd like to have some physical bread to eat like Moses gave to our people during the Exodus.
Jesus: That bread was heavenly bread, and it came not from Moses but from my Father.
People: Sir, if that bread keeps us from starving, we'd like to have you give us that bread always.

The people were confounded by this man saying he has come down from heaven (John 6:41)—this man, Jesus, whose family they know. He was "the son of Joseph whose father and mother we know" (John 6:42). Isn't it interesting that it is Joseph who is named and not Mary? And this carpenter's son coming down from heaven? No way! They said they knew where this man came from, but that would not be true of the Messiah. Furthermore, the scriptures say that the Messiah will not come from Galilee. Being a descendant of David, he will come from Bethlehem, where David lived (John7:41–42). It appears that they had not heard of, or had disregarded, the Nativity story (Matthew 1:18–25 and Luke 2:1–7). And yet, in spite of such opposition, there were still those who loudly declared, "This is the Messiah" (John 7:42).

Now, what to make of all this? When the Fourth Gospel was written at or after the end of the first century, the word *Jews* referred to hostile opponents of the Christian community which was made up of Gentiles, Jewish Christians, et al. The Jews now appeared to be the chief critics of Jesus when he said that he was the bread from heaven (John 6:35).

In all fairness to the Jews, if we had been there and had been one of them, we might have felt the same way. Chosen by God to be his servants and witnesses, the Jews knew the Law and observed all the rules and regulations of Judaism: attending festivals, worshiping in the synagogue and temple . . . they did it all. They took Jesus literally and could not understand how he could be bread from heaven that could be eaten. Then Jesus's metaphors became even more difficult to understand. In order to have eternal life, they would have to eat his flesh and drink his blood (John 6:56). Even the disciples of Jesus, his followers, had trouble deciphering his remarks. "This teaching is difficult, who can accept it?" (John 6:60). And at home, it was just too much for Jesus's own brothers to believe in him (John7:5).

It might help us to understand the "I am" sayings if we see how "I am" answers these three questions: (1) Who Jesus is? (2) What Jesus does? (3) What Jesus wants us to do?

"I Am the Bread of Life"

1. Who Jesus Is

Let's look at the three places in John 6 where Jesus says that he is the bread of life, the living bread.

First, in John 6:35–42, after identifying himself in this way, he says that those who come to him and believe in him will never be hungry or thirsty. He then goes on to say that as the bread of life he has come down from heaven to do God's will. The biggest objection for those who heard him didn't seem to be that he said he was "the bread of life." It was because he said that he had come down from heaven. They said they knew where he came from. They knew his family, his mother and father. How could he now say that he had "come down from heaven"? This is especially interesting because he had just identified himself as the Son of God and that all who believe in him will have eternal life. His listeners however were expressing their disagreement with him because he kept saying that he had come from heaven.

As "the bread of life," Jesus is speaking of spiritual life, one's relationship with God. And he is asserting that the only way to be in a right relationship with God the Father is to be in a faith relationship with him, the Son of God. This permits Jesus to say, "This is indeed the will of my Father, that all who see the Son and believe in him may have eternal life." (John 6:40).

Today people are still questioning the true identity of Jesus. In this scientific age, many believe that there is a God, but draw the line when

Jesus says, "Not that anyone has seen the Father except the one who is from God, he has seen the Father" (John 6:46). Although in the third person, it is quite obvious that Jesus is speaking about himself. For some today, that seems to be a good reason to be highly skeptical about Jesus who lived two thousand years ago, saying that he is the only one who has had a father-son relationship with the Creator. Even so, some of those who are skeptical about the identity of Jesus are still able to say, "I believe there is a God."

It might seem to have been easier for his disciples to say that they believe in Jesus and will be faithful in following him in his mission because he was standing right there in front of them.

But when the Gospel of John was written, Jesus had been gone some seventy years. So there seemed to be good reason for unbelief just as there is today two thousand years later.

And yet there are some today, as there were in John's day, who say that they "have faith in Jesus Christ." These are Christians who confess to having a belief/faith relationship with Jesus that leads to a life of obedience carrying out his mission. They say that they are having this experience because of the Holy Spirit. When pressed to explain, they say that the Holy Spirit is God's contemporary presence of Jesus Christ.

The *second* place where Jesus says that he is the bread of life is John 6:48–50. He makes reference to their Jewish history when Moses led the Exodus out of Egypt. God had saved them from starving by providing the miraculous manna. But Jesus goes on to explain that the true bread is that which comes from his Father in heaven. He says, "This is the bread that comes down from heaven, so that one may eat of it and not die" (John 6:50). He leaves no doubt that spiritual malnutrition has far worse consequences than physical malnutrition.

The *third* time Jesus identifies himself as "the living bread" is John 6:51–56. He explains that the bread he is talking about is his flesh. With that Jesus lost his audience. He seems to make matters worse when he says that in addition to eating the flesh of the Son of Man they must also drink his blood. By doing that, they will have eternal life.

Are these the exact words of the historical Jesus? Probably not. But why then does the Holy Spirit place them here? Probably because by the end of the first century, Christians were celebrating the Lord's Supper, Holy Communion. They were eating the bread and drinking the wine. These words by Jesus were a reminder that when they took these physical foods they were professing his presence in their lives. And that act of worship has continued through the centuries. At the first moon landing, Astronaut Buzz Aldrin took Communion using a chalice he had brought.

Those listening to Jesus wanted straight talk even as we do today. Thus we can understand why Jesus's metaphorical teaching often missed its mark. But when the Holy Spirit enlightens us, we are able to hear Jesus talking to us today. Because of our faith relationship with Jesus Christ, we take the bread and cup at the Lord's Supper and experience the presence of Christ within us. The people to whom John was preaching/teaching probably understood better than the original audience what the Holy Spirit of the risen Christ was saying.

2. What Jesus Does

The Holy Spirit, in explaining who Jesus *is*, also makes abundantly clear what this Son of God, Son of Man *does*. In all of this, it is clear that John wants his Christian audience to know that this Jesus is being presented differently than the Jesus of the Synoptic Gospels.

The Jesus of Matthew, Mark, and Luke certainly did things that no human counterpart would or could do. He healed the sick and injured, restored the dead to life, prayed successfully for what seemed impossible, graphically explained the kingdom of heaven, did the miraculous like walking on water, fed thousands with almost nothing, and predicted events that will happen in the future. All of these events and occasions were performed by a man named Jesus who came from Nazareth. With such a human origin, they were unexplainable and/or unbelievable.

But the Fourth Gospel goes one step further in explaining what Jesus does. "Whatever the Father does, the Son does likewise." And the reaction to such a declaration? "The Jews were seeking all the more to kill him, because he was . . . calling God his own Father, thereby making himself equal to God" (John 5:18–19).

It must have been difficult to hear this man whom everyone knew as the carpenter's son say that he can give life to anyone he wishes and that he has the authority to judge because he is the Son of Man. Although he does not use the word *heaven*, he does say that it is "the will of my Father, that all who see the Son and believe in him may have eternal life" (John 6:40).

If it was difficult for those who heard and lived with Jesus to accept him for who he said he was, what about the Bible-reading person today? For some it may be just too much to accept and believe. For others there may be a middle ground. They accept Jesus as Lord and Savior but they find these words about Jesus doing what God can do just a little too religious. But there are many who recognize that this man who was full *humanity* was also full *deity*. He was a human being, a man, like all other men in Nazareth. He had the same emotions and feelings. This full humanity is displayed in the Synoptic Gospels. However, unlike other human beings, he was also deity. And that is always in the spotlight in the Gospel according to John. It is quite evident that it is the Holy Spirit who is the author of this Gospel. And when one opens one's life to the Son of God today and confesses a faith relationship with him, it is proof that God's Holy Spirit is continuing to be at work.

3. What Jesus Wants Us to Do

When Jesus speaks of his desire for his friends and acquaintances to believe in him, he is not asking them to accept him as some wonder-worker. He is requesting of them exactly what he is asking of us. He is speaking as the Son of God and is asking his fellow human beings to be in a faith relationship with him. This will involve their confessing him to be the one who truly reveals God the Father/Creator. He tells them that in doing that, they will no longer be hungry or thirsty (John 6:55). Did he mean this literally? Of course not. There were many in Jesus's day, as there are today, who were starving and lacking fresh water.

Being devoid of such basic necessities, it was difficult for his friends to understand his words as metaphors. Jesus knew that for his listeners to be in a right relationship with their fellow human beings, they would need to be in a right relationship with God. But his play on words about hunger and thirst only brought thoughts about food and water. And they didn't see Jesus supplying any of these. They only heard strange talk about who he was, and they found it difficult to translate that into spiritual hunger and spiritual thirst.

Even though his life was in danger, Jesus never stopped trying to help people know the one true God. He never ceased telling them that the way to know the Father was to know him, the Son (believe; have a faith relationship). "Anyone who does not honor the Son does not honor the Father who sent him" (John 5:23). It is made clear that "all judgment" has been given to the Son; therefore, the Son must be honored (John 5:22). Such extreme statements as these emphasized in John are clear evidence why his friends, family, and fellow Galilean citizens would hold Jesus at arm's length. In spite of all the opposition, Jesus never ceased to preach and teach that it was God who sent him. He insisted that those who listen and believe will have eternal life (John 6:40). There are times when Jesus speaks of eternal life as almost equivalent to everlasting life. But here, eternal life is in the present tense. This is the life that comes from believing that God has sent Jesus. This is emphasized in John 6:40, when Jesus speaks of himself in the third person as "the Son." He wants his audience to know that it is God's will for people to believe in him. In doing so, they will have a faith relationship with God resulting in an obedient life. This life is characterized as eternal life.

We must always remember that what we are reading was authored by the Holy Spirit and was presented to a congregation about seventy years after Jesus's death and resurrection. What is said in one passage may appear different in another passage. For example we are told that to eat the living bread (identified by Jesus as himself) means that one, "will live forever" (John 6:51). This means living beyond this life and is not the present tense mentioned in John 6:54. These metaphors, of course, have reference to the Lord's Supper, which the Christian people of the church participated in during worship starting at the end of the first century. Jesus says that they are witnessing to their faith relationship with him when they eat the bread and drink the wine at Holy Communion.

What Jesus wants Christians (the church community) to do today is to continue his mission by sharing with others, by words and actions, that Jesus wants to be the Bread of Life in their life. It is their decision to make.

"I Am the Light of the World"

1. Who Jesus Is

In the Synoptic Gospels, Jesus will often do something in order to explain what he is saying. For example, when he heals the man's withered hand, he is saying that it is lawful to do good on the Sabbath (Mark 3:5). But in the Fourth Gospel, when Jesus does something, we always have to ask, "What is Jesus saying?"

Let's look at John 9:1–12, where Jesus encounters a man blind from birth. He puts mud on the man's eyes and tells him to go wash them in a pool. The blind man does so, and his sight is restored. But what was Jesus really saying when he did that? He explains that this man was born blind so that God's works might be seen in him. But why does he say, "As long as I am in the world, I am the light of the world" (John 9:5)? Does the Son of God not affect the world after his resurrection?

These words may imply that Christ's Holy Spirit is always present, even after the Resurrection, and that he is always the light of the world. Or he may have been indicating that his time on earth would soon end. There is an echo of these words of Jesus in John 12:35, "The light is with you a little longer." This is a reference to the shortness of his ministry on earth. He is the light of the world, but his life on earth will soon be cut short.

Jesus declares himself to be the light for the whole world. This means that his revelation of God is not just for the Jews but for everyone on this earth. It means that Christ's restoring our relationship with

God is not just for religious people but for all people: all cultures, all nationalities, all races, all ages, all genders, the poor and rich.

We have some clue to what he means when identifying himself as light by John 5:19–29. As the Son, he does whatever the Father does. That means giving life to whomever he wishes. What it means to be the Light of the World that gives life is best summarized when he says, "Anyone who hears my word and believes him who sent me has eternal life, and does not come under judgment, but has passed from death to life" (John 5:24).

As the Light of the World, Christ enables us to see God as revealed in the Son and then to open our lives to him. We will thus be in a relationship with God, which is a reflection of the Son's relationship with the Father. The Light of the World is now being reflected into our life.

2. What Jesus Does

God has sent Jesus to help us understand how to treat each other, how to treat ourselves, and how to treat our environment. As the Light, Jesus enables us to do each of those things by our being in a faith relationship with him. In the final analysis, what Jesus does is fully dependent upon what we let Jesus do.

It is difficult for us to believe that when Jesus speaks of darkness he is speaking of sin. We do not like to think of ourselves as sinners. We say, "I do the best I can. Sometimes I'm right, sometimes I'm wrong." Darkness most often means being laid off, watching the stock market destroy one's savings, losing a loved one after many years of a shared life, being told by a doctor that the disease is terminal, etc.

When Jesus speaks of darkness, however, he is not speaking of the horrible and bad things of life. He is speaking of our not confessing our need for him who can change or alter those things.

For example, there is the blind man mentioned earlier. He could have said his blindness was his darkness and grumbled his way through life. Instead he trusted in Jesus and opened his life to him. That new relationship wiped away both physical darkness and spiritual darkness.

What a difference there is between the blind man and Judas, who betrayed Jesus. Judas saw his horrible deed of betrayal as his darkness, a darkness that no light could overcome, like the black hole at the center of our Milky Way galaxy, so Judas killed himself. How tragic! He had not trusted the very one who could have taken away his darkness, the one who had chosen him as one of the twelve apostles. He did not ask Jesus to be forgiven. He ignored the Light of the World who overcomes all human darkness.

3. What Jesus Wants Us To Do

There is no doubt that all four Gospels show what Jesus wants from each of us in our contemporary environment. Jesus knows that we live with those who often fall prey to a host of mystical, emotional religions. He knows that some have created their own personal religion. He knows that there are those who have made themselves God. He knows that there are those who do not believe that there is a God.

When Jesus told his followers that they should walk while they had the light (John 12:35), he was referring to his earthly presence, which would soon be cut short. But this passage also applies to us today who have opened our lives to the Light of Christ. We should share that Light with others while we have the light. We are to be Christ's reflectors even though we are far from perfect, often failing, and always depending on his forgiveness. The Lord Jesus may not be with us physically as he was two thousand years ago, but God has permitted the Holy Spirit of Christ to be with us until the end of time. The Light of the World is in our life now, and God expects us to let that Light shine through our own human personalities. That means engaging in his mission. "As the Father has sent me, so I send you" (John 20:21).

There was a famous quote said by a Jewish survivor of the Holocaust in Nazi Germany in World War II. The Holy Spirit seems to be saying that evil will flourish when Christians do nothing. That Holocaust survivor became a Christian after the war.

"I Am the Gate for the Sheep"

1. Who Jesus Is

In John 10:2, 7, and 9, Jesus is both the gate for and the shepherd of the sheep. God is said to be the gatekeeper (John 10:3), who opens the gate and permits Jesus to lead his sheep (Christians, the church) out into the world to follow him. We're told that Jesus's listeners didn't understand what he was saying. If we had been there, we probably wouldn't have either. We have a two-thousand-year span with the Holy Spirit of Jesus Christ illuminating his meaning.

When Jesus identifies himself as "the gate for the sheep" (John 10:7), he is declaring himself to be the Incarnate One who has a faith relationship with the sheep who follow him and carry out his mission. But who are the thieves and bandits that Jesus says came before him and to whom his followers (sheep) did not listen (John 10:1, 8)? We really don't know. This "sermon" (Fourth Gospel) was written at the end of the first century. Looking back some seventy years, the preacher (author) may be thinking of the Jewish hierarchy and leaders who saw Jesus as a Jewish heretic. Or possibly anyone who attempts to enter God's community by any other way than through the Son of God.

The sheepfold spoken of in John 10:1 is probably the Christian community, the church. In AD 100, that community consisted of Christians who had relatives going back to the Lord's earliest days. But there were others in the community who had been Gentile nonbelievers but were now Christians. And still others were faithful Israelites who were now confessing that this fellow Jew was the pinnacle of God's revelation that began with Abraham. Jesus is the gate, the one way into this community. Indeed, he is the very reason for the existence of the sheepfold. But he is also the one who leads the sheep out of the gate into a lifetime of mission.

2. What Jesus Does

The words that Jesus speaks in John 10:1 about the thief and bandit are more clearly understood when we remember that at the end of the first century (when John was written), there were Jews who strongly believed that only the people of Israel were God's chosen people. There were Gentiles and other non-Jews who had their own cryptic spiritual dogmas. Jesus characterizes all such beliefs as coming from "a thief and a bandit" and that only through him can one become a member of the true community of God's chosen people.

Even in our own contemporary world today, we find those who proclaim (often by TV and radio) that the way one behaves will determine one's being saved. God's self-revelation that culminates with Jesus in the New Testament leaves no doubt that to become a part of God's chosen community, one must be in a faith relationship with the Son of God. This must have been especially gut-wrenching to the faithful people of Israel, for this one who is being touted as the only one who has full control over the sheepfold is Jesus, a *Jew*.

The metaphor of the Christian community being referred to as sheep and Jesus being the gate of the sheepfold is intended to help Jesus's listeners better understand his message. But we are told that they didn't comprehend what he was saying. It is more likely that some seventy to eighty years later, the readers/listeners who read/heard these words had a fairly good idea what Jesus meant. Jesus is not only the true revelation of God who alone can call and bring followers into the Christian community (church), but he also leads them out to perform his mission through words and actions.

In the Synoptic Gospels, this is made much clearer when we see the embryonic church personified in the twelve apostles. We see their being called to mission as "fishers of men" (Mark 1:16). We see Peter healing "a man lame from birth" (Acts 3:2). And the result of their preaching? "Many of those who heard the word believed, and they numbered about five thousand" (Acts 4:4).

In AD 90–110, there were many who opposed the Christian faith and often killed those who had a faith relationship with Christ. And so there were some Christians who found it safer to fall away. Thus it was not historically true when Jesus said that the sheep who follow him in his mission will not listen to or follow a stranger (John 10:5). For this reason, at the end of the century, the Holy Spirit is urging his followers to remain faithful.

In John 10:9–10, Jesus says that anyone who enters the sheepfold through him, the gate, will be saved and have abundant life. Jesus's metaphorical explanation clearly indicates that these individuals are a part of Christ's community, the church. Today it is not unusual to hear someone say, "Accept Jesus Christ as your Lord and Savior, and you will be saved," with the implication often being that you will be saved from hell. When Jesus speaks of receiving salvation through him, he means that your sins will be forgiven. He means that you will be reconciled with God; that is, you will be in a right relationship with God because of your faith relationship with his Son. And Jesus is saying that this applies to anyone and everyone. What a great difference from Judaism, where salvation was often spoken of as applying only to Jews through historical events. Jesus was a Jew, but his concept of salvation was at great variance from his own Judaism.

As one might imagine, these unique views of Jesus in his teaching and preaching and healing brought a great division among his Jewish listeners. "Many of them were saying, 'He has a demon and is out of his mind. Why listen to him?' But others were saying, 'These are not the words of one who has a demon. Can a demon open the eyes of the blind?'" (John 10:20–21).

A few years later, the apostle Paul was teaching and proclaiming the truth of Jesus's message even when suffering in a Roman prison. "The

Gentiles have become fellow heirs, members of the same body, and sharers in the promise in Christ Jesus through the gospel" (Ephesians 3:6). All who are members of the Body of Christ have these same marching orders from the Son of God who lives today. We are called to share the good news of God-in-Christ to all who live on this little blue marble, Earth.

3. What Jesus Wants Us to Do

Jesus wants his sheep to recognize his voice, hear his call, and follow him. The billions of people on this little planet Earth today are still invited by the Holy Spirit of Christ to do just that. However, nowhere in his contemporary call to mission does Jesus say that the person who does not hear his voice or ignores his call will not go to heaven but will go to the other extreme. This falsehood is contrary to Jesus's call to serve and not to judge. Those of us today who are Christians are part of the universal church which is comprised of all who have answered Jesus's call to follow him in mission.

When called, we sometimes ask, "What do I get?" rather than "What am I called to do?" Jesus does not ignore the former for he says that those who hear his voice and follow him in mission will be saved, find pasture (peace) and have an abundant life. (John 10:9–10) But his emphasis is always on what we are to do. He wants us to help others to be in a right relationship with God (reconciled) by opening their lives to a faith relationship with Jesus Christ.

Jesus warns us that when we engage in his mission, there may be times when, if we are not paying close attention, we may allow other voices to gently lead us in another direction until we are far astray from our assigned mission. These other voices are blatantly described as strangers, thieves, and bandits (John 10:8). They are often self-centered and concerned for personal gain. "For where there is envy and selfish ambition, there will also be disorder and wickedness of every kind" (James 3:16). Prayer, worship, and a disciplined study of scripture will help us to detect these phony voices when they appear. We must remain faithful to the mission Christ has assigned to us. For we are "the church of the living God, the pillar and bulwark of the truth" (1Timothy 3:15).

"I Am the Good Shepherd"

1. Who Jesus Is

When Jesus spoke to people, he used metaphors, illustrations, and analogies that those who grew crops and raised sheep would understand. His deep love for those who followed him, those for whom he was willing to give his life, is shown when he describes himself as "the good shepherd." The "sheep" are his faithful followers.

We must always remember that this is not one of the Synoptic Gospels (Matthew, Mark, and Luke). In John, the Holy Spirit, speaking through the unknown author at the end of the first century (John 21:24), has Jesus speaking to his followers, who are both Jews and non-Jews. He very aptly describes the faith relationship between his followers (sheep) and himself, "I know my own and my own know me" (John 10:14). He always lets his followers know that their faith relationship with him is a reflection of his relationship with the Father (John 14:7).

In the Synoptics, Jesus appears to relate to people differently than he does in the Fourth Gospel. In Matthew 15:21–28 a non-Jewish Canaanite woman (Gentile) comes to Jesus, calling him "Lord, Son of David," pleading with him to heal her daughter who is desperately ill. He doesn't answer her, and his disciples urge him to "send her away." The woman keeps begging, and Jesus finally says, "I was sent only to the lost sheep of the house of Israel" (Matthew 15:24). She finally kneels before Jesus and cries, "Lord, help me." When Jesus responds by saying you can't take the "children's food and throw it to the dogs," she says,

21

"Yet the dogs eat the crumbs that fall from their masters' tables." Jesus finally acknowledges her faith and heals her daughter. These differences related in Matthew compared to John are vivid evidence of the great change that took place in the fifty years between the Synoptic Gospels and the Fourth Gospel.

Christians in the church today often echo Jesus in Matthew more than they do Jesus in John. The person who is not a Christian (e.g., a Muslim, a Jew, a Hindu, an atheist, an agnostic etc., etc.) is often ignored and sometimes even thought of as someone "not going to heaven." How sad that these Christians cannot echo Jesus, the "good shepherd" and the Jesus who healed the Canaanite woman's daughter.

What a wonderful analogy Jesus gives when he says that his knowing the church and the Christians of the church knowing him (with *know* implying a relationship), is comparable to the relationship that he and the Father have (John 10:14–15). We must always emphasize that this relationship is not just for what we can get God to give us but for us to be obedient as we engage in the same mission as Jesus Christ, the "good shepherd." This call to mission is also linked to the only other New Testament passage where Jesus is called "shepherd." "Now may the God of peace, who brought back from the dead our Lord Jesus, the great shepherd of the sheep . . . make you complete in everything good so that you may do his will" (Hebrews 13:20–21).

2. What Jesus Does

One of the major differences between the Synoptic Gospels and John can be seen in Jesus's death and resurrection. The Synoptics show the Jews' increasing opposition to Jesus and their eventual collusion with the Roman occupiers to bring about Jesus's death. In the Garden of Gethsemane, Jesus prays that he may not have to die.

In John, Jesus is in perfect relationship with the Father and is in control of his death and even his resurrection. "I will be with you a little while longer, and then I am going to him who sent me" (John 7:33). "I lay down my life in order to take it up again. No one takes it from me, but I lay it down of my own accord" (John 10:17–18).

Perhaps it might help to look at what we might call the three Resurrections of Jesus: (1) from water, (2) from the tomb, (3) from the church as the Spirit of Christ.

1. "As he was coming up out of the water, he saw . . . the Spirit descending . . . on him. And a voice came from heaven, 'You are my beloved Son'" (Mark 1:10–11). Following this rising from the water, Jesus felt the need to get away in order to spend some time thinking deeply about all the implications of this event and what they might mean (Mark 1:12–13).
2. "The angel said to the women, 'Do not be afraid . . . He is not here, for he has been raised. . . . Go quickly and tell his disciples, 'He has been raised from the dead'" (Matthew 28:6–7).
3. "You heard me say to you, 'I am going away, and I am coming to you'" (John 14:28). And he has come to us in the Holy Spirit. After the Resurrection, "The disciples rejoiced when they saw the Lord. . . . He breathed on them and said to them, 'Receive the Holy Spirit'" (John 20:20, 22).

"'Church' has no other valid meaning than this: they are disciples who hear and keep the word of Jesus, in whom and with whom the Paraclete (Holy Spirit) abides, leading them into all truth by declaring the things of Christ, who witness as the Spirit witnesses and thus continue the mission of Christ" (*The Gospel according to St. John*, C. K. Barrett, p. 144).

In the Gospel according to John, Jesus speaks more often about his sacrificial death than he does in Matthew, Mark, and Luke. He makes it plain that his death is on behalf of his sheep. These are his followers who have heard his call and carry out his mission. And he makes it quite clear that it is he who is in charge of his death and resurrection. He furthermore states that all of this is in accord with the will of his Father (John 10:17–18). This is quite a distinction from the more historical presentation in Matthew 27:1–2.

3. What Jesus Wants Us To Do

Jesus's first desire is to have people love him. And for them to do that, they must believe in him. This was probably more difficult for the new Christians at the end of the first century, when the Fourth Gospel was written, than it was when the historic Jesus was on earth healing people. When people saw how this man from Nazareth treated people with such great compassion and love, they felt love for him. And that love made it much easier to believe in him.

But some seventy to eighty years later, it was more difficult. To help them in their belief, Jesus explained that he had come from God (John 16:26–28) and that everything he did was in the name of God the Father. This helped many to believe in him. But of course, not everyone believed any more than they do today. This is why the Holy Spirit of Christ, the real author of the Fourth Gospel, has been present the last two thousand years. He speaks to our spirit, enabling us to believe in him and to serve. But just as in his days on earth, today some believe and some do not.

There is a significant corollary to Jesus's desire that we love him. "This is my commandment that you love one another as I have loved you" (John 15:12). And how has he loved them? He has loved them by laying down his life for them. The Christians of the new church at the century's end are urged to love as Jesus loved, to lay down their lives for one another when persecuted by Rome and other religions. They should do this because of their love for one another, for this is what Jesus did when he died on Calvary because of his love for them.

As important as the love for Christ and the love for one another is, it is the mission that Christ is engaged in that is of paramount importance. This is the same mission that Jesus wants his followers to be engaged in. The way this is expressed in John is quite different from the way the First Gospel describes it. Matthew has Jesus saying, "Let your light shine before others, so that they may see your good works and give glory to your Father in heaven" (Matthew 5:16). In John, Jesus says, "I chose you. And I appointed you to go and bear fruit that will last" (John 15:16). Matthew has the disciples doing their mission to glorify

God. In John, Jesus wants them to bear much fruit because they are attached to him, the "true vine."

This Good Shepherd may also have in mind God's people who were called to serve (Ezekiel 34) and failed because they only thought of themselves. And unfortunately, we see that too often today. Instead of engaging in mission ("bearing much fruit"), we are concerned with how God can bless us, enable us to go to heaven, etc. Ezekiel puts it this way in 34:2: "Ah, you shepherds of Israel who have been feeding yourselves! Should not shepherds feed the sheep?"

"I Am the True Vine"

1. Who Jesus Is

If the parable of the vineyard, John 15:1–8, were a musical on Broadway the overture would certainly include Isaiah 5:1–7. This Old Testament passage cites a parable that has a climax showing that God owns a vineyard and that the vineyard is "the house of Israel."

When the curtain goes up in John 15:1, the vineyard is not Israel but Jesus, "the true vine." His Father is still "the vine grower." A big addition to the parable makes it clear that the new community of the church, the Christians, are also the vineyard because they are branches of the vine. It is they who are called upon to "bear much fruit."

The vines in the old vineyard (Israel) failed because they didn't show "justice" and "righteousness" (Isaiah 5:7). It is made clear that the vine branches in the new vineyard fail when they are not connected to the vine (Jesus) and thus cannot bear fruit. And when that vine is referred to as "the true vine" (John 15:1), there seems to be an imputation that there are many false vines with false branches that must be avoided.

Christians today must make certain that we learn what God's Holy Spirit is teaching us from these words in Isaiah and John. Jesus Christ is the vine, the head of the church. We must not confuse our work as branches with the work of the vine. "I chose you. And I appointed you to go and bear fruit, fruit that will last" (John 15:16). As the branches we are called to live Christ's selfless lifestyle, loving and serving others. And while doing that, we must be aware of the false vines, those who may sound like the Lord but clearly are not. They direct the church to do religious things for personal, selfish, and often unscriptural reasons.

At the end of the first century, it was not just Jews who had come to believe in Jesus as the Incarnate Son of God (per the Synoptic Gospels), but Gentiles, Samaritans, and others who were now in the community of the church. Unfortunately, they did not always love one another. Jesus leaves no doubt that they are to "love one another as I have loved you" (John 15:12). And how does he love them? "As the Father has loved me, so I have loved you" (John 15:9). And then to highlight the value of friendship (which the church certainly needed at that time), Jesus tells them that he is their friend (John 15:14). The clear implication is that God wants them to be each other's friend.

2. What Jesus Does

It is sometimes difficult when reading the Fourth Gospel to catch the depth and full meaning of what Jesus is desiring and doing. In the Synoptic Gospels, Jesus says, "Go and make disciples of all nations . . . teaching them to obey everything that I have commanded you" (Matthew 28:19–20). But in the Gospel of John, Jesus speaks in metaphorical and parabolic figures of speech: "I chose you . . . to go and bear fruit, fruit *that will last*" (John 15:16, my italics). He is concerned not only that they carry out their assigned mission but that it will result in increasing numbers of disciples, a growing community of the church. It is evident that God, working through Jesus and Christians, wants the human beings on this little planet Earth to know who he is, and wants them to be in a faith relationship with him that reflects the relationship between the Son and the Father.

It is also quite clear that this mission cannot be accomplished merely by being religious and moral. Continuing his use of vine and branches, Jesus tells them that they must "abide in [him]" if they are to fulfill his calling (John 15:4). As the Christians faithfully meet in worship, hear the Gospel preached, observe Holy Communion, study the scriptures, and pray together, they will be abiding in Jesus and thus able to carry out his mission.

If being in Christ is the primary requisite for carrying out his mission, Jesus makes it clear that this multicultural church he is addressing must be filled with love for one another. For only then can his commandments be adequately carried out. He says that this love may even lead to sacrificing their lives for one another for this is the way he loves them (John 15:12–13).

It is difficult to know what Jesus means when he says, "My Father . . . removes every branch in me that bears no fruit" (John 15:2). There were Christians then, just as there are today in the church, who were more concerned for self than faithfully carrying out Christ's mission. It would appear that they are no longer considered faithful disciples of Christ or members of the church.

It also shows what happens to those who remain faithful in serving Christ. "Every branch that bears fruit he prunes to make it bear more fruit." The Greek word for *prune* also means "cleanse" and is found in the next verse, John 15:3. Jesus then reminds them once again of the only way they can carry out his mission (being fruitful): "Just as the branch cannot bear fruit by itself unless it abides in the vine, neither can you unless you abide in me" (John 15:4).

3. What Jesus Wants Us to Do

The newly forming Christian community, the church, at the end of the first century knows Jesus as "the Holy Spirit of Christ." This contemporary Jesus wants his followers to become his disciples and have a firm faith relationship with him so that they may witness and testify to friends and neighbors about the person and mission of Christ (John 15:4, 16)

Jesus goes to great lengths to let his followers know that their discipleship and faithful service will absolutely depend on their keeping a close and faithful relationship with him. He says to all who now call themselves Christian that "unless [they] abide in [him]" (John 15:4), they will not be able to "bear fruit." They will not be able to carry out the mission he has assigned to them. He makes it quite clear that without a strong faith relationship with him they "can do nothing."

Jesus also speaks of something that goes beyond, or at least is equal to, their spiritual union with him. We might call it the triangle of love (John 15:9, 12).

1. The Father loves Jesus, the Son.
2. Thus the Son loves his disciples.
3. Therefore, these disciples must love one another.

We need to dig a little deeper to understand why this substantive love will not only determine but demonstrate that Christ's mission is being successfully carried out. Almighty God, the Creator of the universe, has incarnated himself in Jesus of Nazareth. To proclaim one's faith in Jesus is to testify that one is experiencing a reflection of Christ's relationship with God. John uses the word *love* to refer to that experience. Jesus probably finds this word needful and appropriate for this disparate group of Christians at the end of the first century.

He then goes on to say that he wants them to bear "fruit that lasts" (John 15:16). Our Lord wants to make sure that these new Christians from many different religious backgrounds will share the gospel with others in such a way that there is no mistaking what a faith relationship with Christ really means. In giving one's life to Jesus, one is confessing to the reality that Jesus is the revelation of the one true God.

Furthermore, this relationship with God through his Son means that Christians have been given an assignment to share with others the love and forgiveness of God even if, in so doing, they lose their own life. "No one has greater love than this, to lay down one's life for one's friends" (John 15:13). Our immediate thought is Jesus's death on the cross. But when this was written there were many Christians who were being killed because they would not forsake their faith and discipleship. And this has been true through the ensuing centuries. It is still true today.

His name is the Reverend Mr. Wang. As pastor of a church in China, he has long opposed openly the government's desire to control the Christian Church. He has now been put in jail with the possibility of execution. And his response? "In this world, in this crooked depraved and perverse world, how do we demonstrate that we are a group of people who trust in Jesus? It is through bodily submission, through bodily suffering, that we demonstrate the freedom of our souls."

"I Am the Resurrection and the Life"

1. Who Jesus Is

We are accustomed to reading the "I am" sayings of Jesus where he identifies himself in poetic figures of speech. In each instance he is presented differently than he is in the Synoptic Gospels. For example, in Luke 14:14 when Jesus speaks of "the resurrection of the righteous," it's almost like he's speaking of heaven. But not so in John 11:1–44, where Jesus is told by Martha and Mary about their brother, Lazarus, "He whom you love is ill." In the first three Gospels, this would presage a quick visit by Jesus and a healing. But not in John, which is the only place we find this incident. Jesus stays where he is for two more days, long enough for Lazarus to die. Sounds cruel? Not really. It will provide Jesus the opportunity he needs to declare and demonstrate his supreme "I am" saying: "I am the Resurrection" (John 11:25; not all translations have *and the life*). In this episode Lazarus may be an important character, but it is Jesus who is the *main* character.

Further evidence that this narrative comes thirty to fifty years after the first three Gospels is found in John11:8. Instead of his fellow Jews loving, respecting, and appreciating Jesus as in Matthew 15:29–31, they are now trying to stone him. Jesus and his disciples enter this hostile territory of Bethany (only two miles from Jerusalem), and there Jesus brings Lazarus out of the tomb . . . alive!

His being brought back to life did not make Lazarus a hero. On the contrary, Lazarus found that his own life, just recently restored, was in great danger. His presence might lead Jews to become followers of Jesus, and more Jews would become Christians. At the end of the first century, Jews who were faithful to their Hebrew faith were hostile to members of the Christian church. John is the only Gospel where Lazarus's resurrection is found.

But now the big question: what does Jesus mean when he gives himself the self-designation, "I am the Resurrection and the life" (John 11:25)? We can find this statement nowhere else, either in the Synoptic Gospels or elsewhere in John. First of all, we must constantly remind ourselves that the Fourth Gospel comes from a preacher who was inspired by the Holy Spirit of Jesus Christ. And so we will find passages where Jesus speaks of the Son of Man in the third person: "[The Father] has given [the Son] authority to execute judgment" (John 5:26–27). This is followed by his speaking in the first person: "I seek to do . . . the will of him who sent me" (John 5:30).

The Jesus in John will often make a salient theological statement that ricochets off a remark by the person with whom he is speaking. When Jesus says to Martha, who is grieving over the death of her brother, Lazarus, "Your brother will rise again" (or "live again"), her response uses the word *resurrection*. Jesus immediately picks up on that and says, "I am the Resurrection and the life" (John 11:23–25).

It is evident that Jesus does not need to convince Martha that Lazarus will live again, because she admits that he will. Jesus then turns the spotlight away from Lazarus to himself. It is through a faith relationship with him who is full deity-humanity that one will have life beyond life on this earth (John 11:26). With the people of Israel in critical danger from Rome, Jesus wants them to know that Caesar may kill the human body, but those who live and believe in the Son of God will live and never die. Those who believed Jesus became Christians.

2. What Jesus Does

When Jesus uses metaphors such as bread, shepherds, vine, etc., it is not too difficult to understand what he is saying to his followers concerning what he is doing for them and why he wants others to join them as his disciples. But what is he telling people he is doing for them when he tells them that he is the Resurrection and the life?

For one thing he speaks of his Resurrection in different ways. In John 7:33–34, he says, "I will be with you a little while longer, and then I am going to him who sent me. You will search for me, but you will not find me." This sounds quite different from John 20:21–22 when, without anyone searching for him, he appears before his disciples after the Resurrection. "Jesus said to them again, 'Peace be with you. As the Father has sent me, so I send you.' When he had said this, he breathed on them and said to them, 'Receive the Holy Spirit.'"

In John 10:17–18, it sounds like he is the one in charge of his death and resurrection. "I lay down my life in order to take it up again. No one takes it from me, I lay it down of my own accord." This does not appear to be the Jesus in John 19:1–3 or the Synoptic Gospels who is arrested, beaten, declared guilty, and killed on a cross.

As everywhere else in the Fourth Gospel, we must remember the historical setting. At the end of the first century the Christian Church was in the process of being formed. The historical Jesus who was being preached and remembered, when "as yet there was no Spirit," was gone. (John 7:39) The contemporary Jesus is now present in the Holy Spirit in the lives of the Christians and the church.

The greatest danger to these Christians was from Caesar in Rome. His forces were the occupying governing authority in Israel. Anyone opposing him verbally and/or physically met with a cruel death. These new Christians needed to hear and believe that if they were killed, they would have eternal life after death: *"Those who believe in me, even though they die, will live"* (John 11:25). And to give added emphasis, Jesus says that anyone who believes in him as the true revelation of God will never die spiritually: *"And everyone who lives and believes in me will never die"* (John 11:26). He says he can declare these things because he was raised from the dead and personifies eternal life: *"I am the resurrection and the life" (John 11:25).*

3. What Jesus Wants Us to Do

The use of the word *beginning* in Mark 1:1 and John 1:1 is an early indicator that Jesus will be presented differently in these two Gospels.

Mark 1:1 has "The beginning of the good news of Jesus Christ, the Son of God."

John 1:1 opens with "In the beginning was the Word, and the Word was with God, and the Word was God." John 1:14 says that "the Word became flesh and lived among us," but the name Jesus does not appear until John 1:17: "Grace and truth came through Jesus Christ."

Mark presents Jesus as a historical person in the early years of the first century CE. He is baptized by John the Baptist, and the Spirit descends upon him (Mark 1:10). Jesus in the Fourth Gospel "is the one who baptizes with the Holy Spirit" (John 1:33), but there is no scene of his being baptized.

Why the big difference? As we have said several times, the Gospel according to John is presenting Jesus to the newly emerging church some seventy to eighty years after the historical Jesus. In this Gospel, Jesus is almost seen as the Holy Spirit of Jesus Christ, no different than the Christ who is with us today.

What the Carpenter from Nazareth wanted from his contemporary disciples was really no different than what Jesus wanted some seventy years later. Some writer or preacher filled with the Holy Spirit is presenting the Son of God to a new generation of Christians. What started as twelve apostles is now the Christian Church.

What Jesus wanted from the embryonic church at the end of the first century was not only what he wanted from his disciples seventy years before that—now, two thousand years later, it is the same mission that he wants from us today. In John 21:19 when Jesus says to Peter "Follow me," Peter knew that he was certainly not saying, "Follow me and you will go to heaven." On the contrary, he had just told Peter that if he insisted on continuing to be a disciple, he would be killed. The faithful response and obedience that Jesus wanted then is what Jesus wants of Christians now. But his commission does not end with, "So good luck." He reminds the Apostles that they are being sent in the very same way that he was sent: "As the Father has sent me, so I send you" (John 20:21). He assures them that their lives will be filled with courage, confidence, and certainty. He says, "Receive the Holy Spirit" (John 20:22). When Jesus was on earth, being both *human* and *deity*, the people knew the *human* Jesus better and understood God through him. After the Resurrection and Ascension, God is better known now through the *deity* of Jesus, the Holy Spirit of Christ, God's Holy Presence.

When Jesus gave his mission assignment to his disciples, he was not trying to make a new religion for a select few. Nor was he trying to reform the Hebrew faith. "Do not think that I have come to abolish the law or the prophets" (Matthew 5:17). The disciples of Jesus were to go to people of all races, nationalities, and religions: "Go into all the world and proclaim the good news [gospel] to the whole creation" (Mark 16:15).

This is the same assignment that the Lord gives to the Christian Church today. The content of that message is brought out in Luke 24:47, "Repentance and forgiveness of sins is to be proclaimed in [Jesus's] name to all nations." God wants us to do that through our *words*. People often say and do things that they eventually know to be wrong, horribly wrong. They cannot forgive themselves. They may even say, "I don't believe that God, if there is a God, can possibly forgive me." A Christian friend needs to remind that person that Peter, who three times denied that he even knew Jesus, was forgiven by Jesus three times. But the gospel is also lived out in our *actions*. That Christian friend who explains the way Jesus forgives must also be the one who forgives someone who says or does something to him/her in a malicious way. The gospel is lived out in both *words* and *actions*.

An important part of a Christian's life is knowing what Jesus says in the Bible. As helpful as it may be, we must not depend solely on someone else's interpretation of scripture that we hear on TV or radio. Jesus says, "Make disciples of all nations . . . teaching them to obey everything that I have commanded you" (Matthew 28:20). The best way to know everything that he has "commanded" is to read Matthew . . . Mark . . . Luke . . . John.

"I Am the Way, amd the Truth, and the Life"

1. Who Jesus Is

If these "I Am" sayings of Jesus were a Broadway production, this would be the last act. All that goes before is echoed and brought to a dramatic conclusion in these words.

From time immemorial the human species on this little planet Earth has intuited that that there was some Force outside of and beyond them. This something was responsible for the physical nature all around: plants, forests, rivers, oceans, fish, animals, the sun, moon, stars, etc. This something needed to be placated and worshiped because everyone's food and well-being depended on it.

Then some two thousand years ago, along came a young unassuming Jewish carpenter who put the capstone to the search for that something. He was so bold as to say, "If you know me, you will know my Father also. From now on, you do know him and have seen him. . . . Whoever has seen me has seen the Father. I am in the Father and the Father is in me" (John 14:7, 9–10). There was no doubt that this young man, possibly in his late twenties or early thirties, was saying that the One who had been ingratiated to by humans for centuries was now standing before them, proclaiming self-identification. He said, "I am the way. . . . No one comes to the Father except through me" (John 14:6).

The Fourth Gospel opens with "In him was life, and the life was the light of all people" (John 1:4). This young Jewish preacher-teacher

39

eventually meets a Jewish religious leader, a Pharisee named Nicodemus. Nicodemus visits Jesus secretly at night. When he confesses his admiration of Jesus's ministry, Jesus says that one must be "born of the Spirit" (John 3:8) to really understand who he is. When Nicodemus continues to confess his lack of understanding, Jesus doesn't seem to help things when he refers to himself as "the Son of Man," and he then adds to the Jewish leader's confusion by saying, "Whoever believes in [the Son of Man will] have eternal life" (John 3:15). Jesus is not saying that "eternal life" is our life beyond this life in heaven. He is speaking of our present life when we acknowledge and confess that God is revealed in Jesus Christ. We live in relationship with God through our faith relationship with Jesus. Nicodemus must have gone home that night muttering to himself as he went to bed and probably didn't get much sleep. But it's interesting to note that later on, we find that he is always on Jesus's side.

Jesus's closest disciples were often as confused as Nicodemus.

When Thomas and Philip asked him some questions of deep concern, Jesus gave them a complete and composite answer: "I am the way, and the truth, and the life" (John 14:6).

2. What Jesus Does

Jesus identified himself as the way, truth, and life because he knew that only as his disciples understood him for who he was could they carry out his mission after he left this earth. This is also true for his followers in the Christian Church today. He is not just the founder of one of the world's great religions or any other common title. He identifies himself by telling us what he does. And he tells us what he does because of who he is.

When Jesus says that he is the Way (John 14:6), he is explicitly saying that through him—and only through him—can one be in a spiritual relationship with God. "No one comes to the Father except through me" (John 14:6). Putting it a little more plainly, he says, "If you know me, you will know my Father also" (John 14:7). To put it even more plainly: "Whoever has seen me has seen the Father" (John 14:9b). And then to put a closing exclamation point, he says, "Believe me that I am in the Father and the Father is in me" (John 14:11).

If Jesus were here today with us as he was two thousand years ago, he would find the same questioning and unbelief as he found then. To begin with, how can one who is human also be deity? Unthinkable.

Besides there are many other concepts about who the mighty Creator-Judge may be. And those concepts include ways to appease the Creator so as to be in a safe relationship with him, When Spain began its conquest of Mexico in the fifteenth century, they found native peoples who had strong beliefs about the mighty force that controlled them. The natives violently opposed these invaders who brought with them this strange Christian belief. Today there is still strong opposition throughout the world. A study has shown that 80 percent of persecuted religious believers are Christians. In some countries, to confess one's Christian faith can bring death. Of course, there are always those who oppose any belief in a Creator responsible for the universe, like Carl Reiner, the Hollywood actor, who said, "God is us,"

As Jesus provides the *way* to God, he also enables us to live a lifestyle in the *way* that he did. This way of life by Christ's followers demonstrates not only who he is but what he requires. The faith relationship that the Christians have with the Holy Spirit (Christ with us now) enables them to carry out the mission that Christ has assigned. It is a continuation of his earthly mission. This means that going to church and/or pledging is not enough. Those who follow Jesus show whether or not they are living the Jesus way by the way they live their daily lives.

When Jesus says that he is "the truth" (John 14:6), he is saying, "If you know me, you will know my Father also" (John 14:7). Through him we know the one true God. Even for his believers, these words were often a bridge too far. His fellow Jews felt they knew God by worshiping with others and reading their scriptures (our Old Testament). When Jesus told them "I am in the Father and the Father is in me" (John 14:10), he hit a very tender religious nerve.

It leads the people to ask, "Who is this man?" (John 5:12; 7:12,15). He answers, "I am life" (John 14:6). By that he is referring to more than being with his followers in their daily living environments. He speaks of true life that one has only when in a right relationship with God. And Jesus is never hesitant in explaining that such a relationship can only exist through faith in him. And he is quite clear as to how people can relate to him after he has left this earth. He says, "I will not leave you orphaned" (John 14:18). "He said this about the Spirit, which believers in him were to receive; for as yet there was no Spirit, because Jesus was not yet glorified" (John 7:39). The people who heard these words read and preached in 100 CE knew what Jesus was talking about. These Christians knew that he was present with them. "You know [the Spirit of Truth], because he abides with you, and he will be in you" (John 14:17). He wraps it up with "The Advocate, the Holy Spirit, . . . will teach you everything and will remind you of all that I have said to you" (John 14:26). And the Beloved Disciple who personifies the Holy Spirit of Christ is doing that in Fourth Gospel.

3. What Jesus Wants Us to Do

Jesus is always crystal clear about what he wants his followers to do. Their mission is to be a continuation of his mission and is the equivalent of doing these things for him.

"I was hungry and you gave me food, I was thirsty and you gave me something to drink, I was a stranger and you welcomed me, I was naked and you gave me clothing, I was sick and you took care of me, I was in prison and you visited me" (Matthew 25:35–36).

When the twelve apostles received this commission, *"They went out and proclaimed that all should repent. They cast out many demons, and anointed with oil many who were sick and cured them." (Mark 6:12–13).*

Christians who continue his mission today show by their *words* and *actions* that Jesus is the one true revelation of God and there is no other. He is present today in the Holy Spirit. (It is unfortunate that the fourth century Nicene Creed that is still used today almost makes the Trinity appear to be three Gods: "And we believe in the Holy Spirit . . . who with the Father and the Son together is worshiped and glorified.")

The way that we are able to accomplish Jesus's mission today is far different than the way they did at the end of the first century: TVs, radios, films, computers, etc. But the environment in which that mission is carried out may not be that different. As we have already said, there are more people being persecuted throughout the world today because they are Christians than of any other spiritual belief. At the end of the first century, when these words of the Fourth Gospel were being written/preached, Rome was killing multitudes of Christians because of their opposition. Many were put on crosses and burned to death. Here in the United States, we do not face such danger as Christians do in other countries, but when we speak and/or live out our faith in Christ, we sometimes face strong opposition. This is when we need to remember how Jesus responded to his fellow Jews when they derided him as some kind of heretic, sometimes opposing him violently. He never backed down on his message or made it more shallow to be acceptable. He continued to try to correct his opposition, and . . . he never stopped loving them.

Today, even though the Holy Spirit of Christ wants us to be firm in our faith, we Christians too often are apt to back down. Our motto seems to be "To each his own." One reason for this may be that we really don't know the scriptures very well. We may have forgotten that being a Christian is not just being someone who believes in Christ hoping to go to heaven; it is being a follower who has been called to mission.

A Broadway star who is a Christian recently led his audience in the Lord's Prayer. In a later interview, he said, "You get more spiritual as you grow older. You're closer to the other world, so maybe that has something to do with it."

The call is to mission and not to being "more spiritual." The object is doing Christ's work on earth and not concentrating on heaven, which awaits. Therefore we must ask ourselves these two questions: (1) Do I really understand the full significance of Jesus's call to mission? (2) If I respond affirmatively, will it be for some personal gain? Like the man in Matthew 19:16–22, who asked Jesus what he must do to go to heaven. When Jesus told him what he had to do, he said, "Thanks, but no thanks."

Jesus is not asking us to be some super spiritual individual, for there is no such person. But when we do slip in our faithfulness, we must remember the apostle Peter who denied three times that he even knew Jesus. Yet he repented . . . and was forgiven . . . and continued serving the Lord (John 21:15–19).

Therefore let it be said of us as it was of Jesus's disciples: *"They went out and proclaimed the good news everywhere, while the Lord worked with them and confirmed the message by the signs that accompanied it"* (Mark 16:20).

The End? Just the Beginning

The Christian Church has a history, and the twenty-first century church has a continuing role in that history. Just as every human being on earth is a product of their genetic past, so it is that the church's DNA comes through Jesus's twelve apostles. But the church today that has that DNA often behaves far differently than that early church.

Jesus's teaching of who he is, what he does, and what he wants us to do has often been lost in Christian hatred, war, slavery, racism, etc. One sad example of this is the seven major Crusades from 1096 to 1291. The church's military force attacked the Muslims who governed the Holy Land. This resulted in retaking Jerusalem, but Christian control of the Holy Land only lasted a few years. So more military Crusades and killing continued for another 104 years. The result was Christians' hatred and distrust of the Muslims, and Muslims of the Christians.

How different from Jesus who, when his mission was confronted with violent opposition, responded with courage, determination, understanding, patience, and . . . love (Matthew 5:44). What we overlook today is that Jesus, in the person of the Holy Spirit, is still assigning his mission to the Christian Church. Unfortunately, Christians too often replace the Spirit-directed mission with homegrown "religion": being moral . . . feeling good and being happy . . . working to achieve heaven . . . ignoring or opposing anyone who disagrees with us . . . loving and forgiving others who love and forgive us. When the Holy Spirit of Jesus Christ calls us to follow him today, it is a call to be with him in mission. And in following him, we do not follow the Jesus we want him to be. This is the Son of God revealed in the Gospel of John by the Holy Spirit who tells us: who Jesus is, what Jesus does, and above all, what Jesus wants us to do. This is the story of the birth and newborn years of the Christian Church. It is we who determine the identity of the Christian Church today and what it will be in the future.

Addendum

The year was 1938. It was a play before a theater audience showing events taking place in a small town between 1901 and 1913. The author of *Our Town* was Thornton Wilder. The main character is the Stage Manager, who speaks to the audience throughout the play, introducing characters, explaining events, etc.

On occasion, the Stage Manager even gets into the play, taking the role of a character.

It may seem strange to say that *Our Town* almost appears to reflect what we have found in the Fourth Gospel. Let's look at it this way.

The one telling the story
- *Our Town*: Thornton Wilder
- Gospel of John: the writer/author (preacher?)

The years when the drama occurred
- *Our Town*: some twenty-five to thirty-five years before
- Gospel of John: about seventy to eighty years before

The one presenting the events of the drama
- *Our Town*: the Stage Manager
- Gospel of John: the Holy Spirit

Roles taken in the story
- *The Stage Manager*: minister, shop owner, townsman, etc.
- *The Holy Spirit*: the Beloved Disciple

The last act of *Our Town* deals with death and eternity. The Gospel of John concludes with the death and resurrection of Jesus Christ, who says, "As the Father has sent me, so I send you. . . . Receive the Holy Spirit" (John 20:21–22).

Index

A

apostles, vii, 13, 17, 36, 42, 45

B

Beloved Disciple, vii–ix, 42, 47. *See also* Holy Spirit

C

Caesar, viii, 34–35
Christian Church, 10, 15, 17, 19, 22–23, 27–29, 31, 34–37, 40, 45–46
Crusades, 45

E

eternal life, 1, 3, 5–6, 8–9, 12, 35, 40

F

faith relationship, 5–10, 12, 15–18, 21, 28–30, 34, 40–41
false vines, 27

H

Holy Communion, 7, 10, 28
Holy Spirit (*see also* Beloved Disciple), viii–ix, 6–9, 11, 13, 15, 17–18, 21, 23–24, 27, 29, 34–37, 41–43, 45, 47–48
humanity, 8, 34

I

Isaiah 5:1-7, *27*

J

Jesus Christ
as the Bread of Life, 5–10
as the Gate for the Sheep, 15–19
as the Good Shepherd, 21–25
as the Light of the World, 11–13
as the Resurrection and the Life, 33–37
as the True Vine, 27–30
as the Way, the Truth, and the Life, 39–44
Jews, viii, 2, 7, 11, 16–17, 21–22, 28, 33–34, 41, 43
John (Gospel)
5:19–29, *12*
6:35–42, *5*
6:48–50, *6*
6:51–56, *6*
9:1–12, *11*
10:9–10, *17, 18*
11:1–44, *33*
14:6, *39, 40, 41*
15:1–8, *27*
Judas, 13

49

L

Lazarus, 33–34
Lord's Supper, 7, 9
love, 24, 29
  triangle of. *See* triangle of love

M

Matthew 15:21-28, *21*
metaphors, 2, 9, 16, 21, 34
mission, 6, 10, 13, 15–19, 22–25, 28–30,
    36–37, 40–43, 45
moon landing, 7

N

Nicodemus, 40

O

Our Town, 47–48

R

Resurrection, the, viii, 11, 23, 33–35, 37
Rome, viii, 24, 34–35, 43

S

Synoptic Gospels, vii, ix, 1, 7–8, 11, 17,
    21–22, 28, 33–35

T

triangle of love, 30

Printed in the United States
By Bookmasters